DEDICATION

This book is dedicated to my daughter. My mini-me.
My reason for being,

She inspires me to be better every single day.

Lyrically Speaking

Ms. Paradox

ISBN: 978-0-9932597-0-8

CONTENTS

ACKNOWLEDGMENTS

Firstly I would like to acknowledge the Unseen, Ubiquitous
Force that inhabits my mind, body and soul when I write.

I am forever grateful to have been blessed with this gift.

I would also like to acknowledge my amazing support network
who build me up, support my dreams and accept me.

Whether near or far, here or gone, I acknowledge YOU

Sweet N Short Soliloquys

Sweet and short soliloquys is a collection of pieces
that I started writing in 1998.

The tone of my voice has changed and matured as
have I. But the focus remains the same.
Love, Life and Lyrics

LOVE WITHOUT BOUNDARIES

Love is complete, and without boundaries.
There are no maybes in love and no waiting around for a sign or waiting for it to grow.
When you're in love you know.
Doubts fall away and you're stripped bare with only your heart to guide you because your head cannot comprehend the majesty of love.
When you love someone it is all encompassing and all consuming.
It is the acceptance of every facet of the other's being, a meeting of minds, bodies and souls.
True love requires no effort and transcends petty arguments and disagreements.
True love is pure in its simplicity.

COMPLEX LOVE

Love is incredibly complicated.
It steals your heart, takes your breath away and leaves you lost for words.
But true love provides gains which far outweigh the loss!
Love hard and love strong

INSATIABLE

That feeling when you can't keep your hands off someone when suddenly a flash of understanding passes between you and you just can't imagine not doing it again. Kissing just keeps going and going, conversation flows, soft caressing in the dark..........

YEARNING

Sometimes I sit here and all I yearn for is to talk to you, not about anything major, just the little stuff, the quirky things that happened during the day.

The people who annoyed me, the things that made me smile. But I can't tell you and that hurts. You made falling in love the hardest and easiest thing for me to do.
"I found in you an endless love" that transcends time and space

xxxxxxxx

DUPLICITOUS LOVE

Love is a double edged sword
A wonderful yet painful thing
To love is to receive and give of yourself

Yet loving opens people up to a
Wider array of emotions which
Sometimes brings pain

TRUE LOVE?

Love is the ultimate union of two people
True love that is.
True love, although it can be interrupted
Cannot be ended, erased or killed.

It lives on forever
Through all eternity
Through life and death

ATTRACTION

Physical attraction
The meeting of two bodies
Inexplicable attraction
The meeting of two minds

Which is better?
One does not know
To fulfill the body?
To fulfill the soul?

URGES

Uncontrollable urges to be with you
Physical attraction
Leading to inexplicable attraction
A touch prompts a thought
All thoughts lead to you

PARTS OF A HEART

You can't split an atom
Can you split a heart?
Are there partitions and sections?
Or just the one thing?
For one person?

THE UNION

Hugging and kissing and laughing and caressing
The feel of hot bodies totally pressing
Against each other heartbeat to heartbeat
The union of two as they feel complete

SKIN TO SKIN

The feel of my breast
Upon his warm chest
To be feeling this good
I must have been blessed

ENCOUNTERS

First encounters come just once
But memories last forever

SUDDEN INSPIRATION

You bring a ray of sunlight
On those dark and cloudy days
You bring a smile to my eyes
And warmth to my heart
Your friendship does nothing but amaze

ANTICIPATION

His words are like a sweet caress
Like silk across my face
For his eyes I will undress
When we reach that special place

YOU

Aching for you
And the things that we share
The lives we have together
The tenderness and care

Waiting for the time
To show my love again
To release pent up emotion
And erase all this pain

Pain that time apart has caused
And that time together will heal
Until we're together, I'll continue to ache
For your sight, your smell, your feel

So forget me not
I say to you
For the time is at hand
When we again shall be two

YOU FOR ME

Everyone searches for that special person
The one who shares their rhythm
The match to their candle
The one who sets them alight
One touch sets my skin on fire
The slight smile that tells me what you're thinking

BLOWN AWAY

You blow me away
Just catching your eye
And holding your gaze
Moves me beyond reason

My breath catches
And I am lost
The rest of the room disappears
You enchant and engage me

WHAT IS LOVE

The concept of love changes
Time and age alter perception
Back then love was simple
For love was misunderstood
Love appeared to be a feeling
A sense of sharing and caring

Now I know that love is different
It has many sides
Deep and shallow
It is about the good and the bad
Rolling with the blows
And savoring the kisses

Love is proved by what happens in the darkness
Not what happens when everything is bright
I love him, will not leave him
I will cherish him, protect him
And hope it lasts forever

UNITED

As the teardrops rain down on my face
And as your back turns
Making the inevitable journey out of this place
My heart is breaking

Your spirit is troubled by my sadness
And mine yearns to appease you
I want you to understand the ache
To understand how my heart strains to be with you

My urge for a baby will give life to us
Will be the ultimate commitment
The ultimate seal and bond
Between you and I
As two become one

ONE NIGHT STAND

You lay deep in the cave that I call my mind
Stirring at times
But mainly dormant
A wisp of a memory
That I'm longing to find

To remember your touch and how you sound
Savouring the memory of how you smelled
I yearn to feel you again
For this thirst to be quelled

But I know that our time
Is way in the past
A one time tryst
That was over too fast

Letters from the Heart

Sometimes when I am overcome by emotion and feel unable to express myself directly I pen secret letters to those who are close. I may not be able to say the words but my letters help me manage my emotions.

LETTER TO MY DADDY

"To feel loss is a human trait, I wish I wasn't human"

Dear Daddy

I just wanted to wish you a safe and enjoyable journey.

I wish it wasn't a journey that you had embarked on right now but alas such is life and death.

Through all this heartache and sadness I can't help but smile as I imagine you reminiscing and revisiting old friends and haunts that punctuated your life.

You always had a way of regaling us with tales of your adventures and I especially looked forward to when you were with Uncle Compton and Nevlyn where jokes would abound.

I will miss your quick wit and humour and your special way of laughing at your own jokes.

Over the years our shared sense of humour and irreverence enabled us to transcend the father/daughter relationship and build a strong friendship based on mutual respect played out through dry and often inappropriate jokes.

Our tit for tat has now come to an abrupt end and surprise surprise you won.

I can't believe that you are gone I didn't even pack for this occasion despite you spending every year since my fifth birthday telling me it would be your last.

The only other time you surprised me is when you bought me a Valentine's Day card and inscribed it with the words "wonders never cease but daily increase".

So I leave you now with the knowledge that you were the 8th wonder of my world.

Love you Daddy
xxxxxxxxxx

LETTER TO MY MOTHER

Dear Mum

I didn't know until the day that I became a mother.
I couldn't love so strong or fierce for any one or other.

A mother's love is uniquely flawed.
Senseless in its strength
Designed to go through pain and joy
To make you go through any length

Mummy is the strongest word
That I have ever heard
A word to make you feel as if
You're soaring like a bird

Mummy is the one you ask
When questions get too tough
Mummy always gets it done
No matter smooth or rough

Mummy, mummy, mummy like music to my ears
Mummy, mummy, mummy, you take away my fears

Lots of love
ME

LETTER TO MY FIANCE

Dear C

I miss you a lot today. It feels like the time since I have seen you is forever. So I wrote this for you.

When the sun goes down
And I'm not there
Think of me
I'm thinking of you

When you open your eyes to the morning sun
And I'm nowhere near
Think of me
I'm thinking of you

Although not together
We're always close
In each other's hearts
In each other's souls

So in every waking moment
And every single breath
Think of me
I'm thinking of you

xxxx

LETTER TO MY DAUGHTER

Hello Little One

How are you doing?

I wonder if you will ever know that it is you who saved me. Paradoxically you are the one who gave me life. You are the reason I keep living day after day keep putting one foot in front of the other and carrying on.

Even when things are bad and I am in a tailspin of emotion and a maelstrom of unhappiness and uncertainty you ground me. You pull me from the brink because in you I see the future. In you I see a power that I can only watch in awe.

You are my responsibility. It is my job to help you achieve the potential that lies within your tiny soul. You saved me my child. From the darkness that beckoned. From the grim reaper who often smiled beguilingly, willing me to take his hand and journey to the depths of hell. But in you I found my light. The chink of light that reminded me of all that is good.

I will never burden you with looking after my soul or actively making me stay but I look at your face and thank the spiritual ruler for giving me a sign. For helping me think beyond myself.

So little girl take the world by its horns. Twist and turn it and make it yours. Aim beyond the stars and know I will always be here to support you and guide you on this journey called life.

Forever yours

Mummy x

LETTER TO MY FRIENDS

Dear Friends

You're in my life because I make a choice
To offer you my time
I won't always be accessible or on the phone
Hope that's not a crime

Friends for me are not a need
Not something that I crave
I won't make up no rules or make a list
Of how you should behave

Some things I do need from my friends
Include
No bullshit, drama or hating
Acceptance and reciprocity
Not conflict and pointless debating

I give to you a hand my friend
For us to share this journey
It's us together till the end
On that we can agree

Ms. P x

LETTER TO MYSELF

Hey Girl

How you doing?

You've had a hard few years. Lots of ups and downs but guess what? You got through them.

No matter how hard and dark things may have got you stuck it out. You kept going!

So here's some advice for you:

- Forgive yourself; I don't know what perceived crimes you are punishing yourself for but you must move on.

- Let yourself remember. I know that some experiences over the years almost broke you. I know you struggled with darkness but shutting those feelings off isn't the answer. Let the memories wash over you. Secure in the fact that they can't hurt you.

- Trust yourself. You are an A grade expert in you. So why not trust the specialist and start hearing what you say.

Love You, Me, Myself and I

Spitting from the Soul

One of my creative influences is music. These pieces draw on the worlds of hip hop and rap and have an edgier tone and provocative lyrics.

Not for the faint hearted.

LYRICAL BITCH

I'm a lyrical bitch
I feel what I spit
The things that I say
Capture your soul
Then blow you away

Come take my hand
While I rock this joint
Words flow relentless
While I'm making my point

Restless energy
Like a dog with an itch
Remember I said
I'm a lyrical bitch

BAD GIRL

Used to be a sub
But that shit is done
Imma take control use you
For my fun
This is my world now
You better believe

I got gadgets and toys and tricks up my sleeve
You wanna use me for pussy
Well baby I'm down
Ain't no other bitch be taking my crown

Fuck me hard
Fuck me raw
Then let me take you
On my tour

First stop is the neck
To lick n to bite
Then it's the titties a glorious sight
Then look at my booty
Use your hands to explore
Before we end at the treasure
My pussy galore

QUEEN BEE

Many have tried to take my Crown
Wannabe bitches who thought they were down
But 19 years on
And we're still not done
Guess that means I'm number ONE!

ADDICTION

The devil is inside me
The devil knows my name
He knows what I am feeling
He sees inside my pain

The devil is my keeper
I know that he's in charge

The devil is my husband
And I'm his lowly wife
The devil is beside me
Till I leave this lonely life

JEZEBEL

Am I a jezebel?
I think that I am
He says I can't have him
I think that I can

I watch him and hunt him
He is my prey
It's the things that I do
Not the things that I say

It's a subtle seduction from our first introduction

I twinkle my eyes
And flutter my eyelids
Eyeing my prize
Like an auction's bid

Now time has passed
I've had a small taste
No thoughts of decency
No time to be chaste

I really don't like him
Our time here is done
I've made his heart want me
I've had all my fun

I know I'm a hussy
And I have no shame
He's a fool for my love
All part of my game

NOT YOURS

You thought you could break me
You were holding me back
I remember the smile
And jokes you would crack

Trying to break me
Make me unsure
Make me dependent
Make me your whore

But I am not yours
I am mine
Not anyone else's
And I'm perfectly fine

No more you
No more us
Just me
With minimal fuss

MS P RECIPE

Fire and ice
Bad but nice
That's what Ms. Paradox is made of

She's cool but she's hot
A pushover she's not
That's what Ms. Paradox is made of

She enchants and entrances
Why not take your chances
To find out what Ms. Paradox is made of

OBSESSED

An obsessive mind is never done
Thoughts racing like bullets from a gun
Night means nothing
When obsession calls
Waiting for the point of it all

Sleep ain't my friend
Sleep is my foe
Need to empty my mind
Make it go slow

Capture these thoughts
Inside of my head
Arrange them on paper
Till they lay down like they're dead

Counting the time
Till I should be awake
All the things to be done
Money to make

Now dawn is breaking
I been up all night
Time to make money
Cos my game is real tight

.

Life Support

I've been through a lot of ups and downs in my life and I used all sorts of tools to help me get through. This section is about how I manage the good and bad times

SISTER FRIENDS

This is for all the sister friends
Who share all the drama
From the start to the end
No drama too big
No drama too small
From a broken nail
To why didn't he call?

Sister friend is there
Through ups and through downs
She becomes just an ear
When you need her the most.
So pick up the phone
Give sister friend a call
Read this to her
Tell her it all

She's a friend
She's a sister
A listening ear
Offer yourself
Let her know
You'll be there

For her ups and her downs
Through thick and through thin
Wherever you are
Sister friend has been
Never forget your sister friend
She was there at the start
She'll be there at the end

BETRAYAL

I was out at a party with some of my friends.
Bet you can't tell how this story ends.

I ended up stranded, no place to go.
He offered me help, I didn't know.

The help that he offered came with a price.
When we got to his house he told me be nice.

I didn't want to I told him f@£(off.
But I couldn't maintain it, acting so tough.

So I stopped trying to fight. I completely gave in.
What he did next was the ultimate sin.

I didn't leave I was too afraid
So I lay there for hours awake and just stared.

When it was light I dressed and I left.
My heart was heavy I was completely bereft.

But I still couldn't scream it wouldn't come out
When he kissed me goodbye I wanted to shout.

It wasn't ok, you took what was mine.
But he smiled at me like it was totally fine.

That was a long time ago I don't talk bout it much.
Took me awhile not to flinch from a touch.

Now I know I was right he was wrong.
Wish it hadn't taken so long.

I was raped. No other word.
To say anything else would JUST be absurd!

THE AFTERMATH

I knew it when I felt it
The moment I unravelled
It didn't happen overnight
It happened some years later

I started taking chances
Became bold in my advances
Chasing men and acting up
And falling out of dances

The beginning of the end it was
When I met my green eyed lover
Could have made it to his house
But somehow thought why bother

Out in the open feeling night's cold air
Not caring or concerned with other people's stares

Dress up
Pants down

My moan
His groan

Full then empty
Pleasure then pain

My loss
His gain

The Dark Side

To appreciate the light we must understand the dark.
I have a dark side.
I have been to the dark side.
I do not inhabit the dark side but I definitely visit
occasionally

SCREWED UP

Where is my life?
All screwed up in tatters
When I look at it clearly
My heart just shatters
I can't take it much longer
Imprisoned by pain
Your life has gone on
I can see that's quite plain
You didn't leave your love and your life
So you don't understand what's causing me strife

PAIN

I release my pain by crying tears
As I think of my hopes, my dreams. My fears

Not knowing what is to come

Or where I shall be
Not able to look after the one named me

I want to be home
Living a life I enjoy

Not stuck here in England
Under the White man's employ

All I need is a listening ear
But when I call out there's no one there

I know I have family who love me a lot
But what of friends and others to listen?
I must say that no one have I got

UNCERTAINTIY

I'm taking an effortless ride down the path of uncertainty
A road fraught with indecision and seemingly unanswerable
questions
The end appears from here to be blurred
Hopefully the closer I get
The clearer it will be
What will be in the hazy horizon called the future?

ALONE

Today I feel so lonely
So alone
Why am I the type of person that attracts the loneliness?
Being alone has become a skill
I don't mean literally alone
I mean alone inside
The people I let in don't seem to want to stay
Why can't words be forthcoming to end the loneliness?
Am I selfish?
Am I spoilt?
I don't think so, just lonesome and alone, with no one

MORE PAIN

I sit here crying
Trying yet again to release the pain
I am always wondering whether there is something wrong
with me
More importantly what IS wrong with me?
Like King Midas I have a special touch
But the difference is that everything I touch turns to dust

ALONE AGAIN

What pain separation brings!
I am yet again left "alone"
I feel so insecure
I don't know why I am always just alone
What is it about me that makes people think that I am strong enough to take this pain over and over again?

I try to let people in hoping that they will have some compassion, not sympathy, just the ability to go easy on me.
Instead their concern is merely momentary.
Quickly overtaken by their own lives

THE DARKNESS

I look at my life and the way I feel right now.
I look all around me but there's no one to talk to
Everything is buried so deep down inside.
I can't imagine how good it would feel to let it all out
I know most people who read this would say I am wallowing in self-pity
Maybe I am, but it is so hard when I can't find the light at the end of the tunnel.
I am just surrounded by darkness.
Sometimes I wish the darkness would envelop me and I could surrender myself to it just floating in the darkness being welcomed by its inviting arms

DARKNESS BECKONS

Darkness exists in my subliminal mind
Like a cloud full of rain
It hovers
Darkness beckons like a welcoming hand
Offering an emptiness to get rid of the pain
Darkness looms, scary yet familiar
Lurking in the corners and crevices of my inner self
Darkness is there when the light offers nothing
The dilemma is whether to accept or to fight

DEAD OR ALIVE

What would death feel like?
An ultimate euphoria or a let down?
Would I finally be at peace?
Or would my soul still feel tormented?
Would my tears cease?
Or would I be forced to have an eternity of crying?

DEPRESSED

Depressed I lay upon the bed
Crying lonely tears
My heart could not fight again
I'd succumbed to all my fears

Depression is a cold and dark
And lonely awful jail
Designed to keep you trapped inside
To make you like a snail

Carrying your woes and ills
Upon your back forever
Never able to shake it off
Ties that you can't sever

Depression is a formidable foe
An enemy like no other
It will take you from you family
Your wife, your dad, your mother

So fight hard my soldier
Do it for me your ever loving wife
Choose light and happiness above all else
Make sure that you choose life

KNIVES

When it's dark
The knives come out
Ready to cut my flesh
The cutting up and down they do
Takes away my stress

The rhythm of the slicing goes
Up and in and out
At first the pain was too much
It made me want to shout

But I got used to feeling pain
In a way it was much better
Than all the pain inside my head
And so I'm writing you this letter

To let you know that I'm ok
With my cuts along my arm
It's my technique for coping now
It's really not self-harm

ANGER

The shower is on
I can hear the water fall
You're spent now
Anger dissipated.
I'm in our room
Tending my wounds
Arm bruised
Face sore
Don't know if
I can take anymore
You say it won't
Happen again
The beating and slaps
Teasing and taunts
I believe you
Less and less
Each time
You hit me again

PERMISSION

I'll never forget the first time I heard it
Whispered in hushed tones
He'd taken a life
It was his own

Suicide came calling at my family's door
Suicide isn't mindful of the rich or the poor
Suicide a word not to be said
Suicide means that someone is dead

When you hear that word young
It does something within
It gives you permission to commit it, a sin

Suicide runs through veins like the blood
Suicide is in our DNA
Wouldn't you say?

Over the years more of us tried
But lucky for us
None of us died

The legacy must stop
Can no longer live on
What would we do if any of us were gone

Let's end the cycle
Start a new family norm
Learn how to cope
How to weather the storm

Let's share our stories to make this curse end
Let's help each other to be on the mend

It's not a word I use in my house
Not even whispered as quiet as a mouse

My little girl won't ever think it's a choice
That's one evil I won't give a voice

Musings

I'm an opinionated woman. Full of views that
sometimes spill over into my creative pursuits.
So I present to you Musings.
My take on the world, random and rambling.

TODAY aka THE COACHES' CREED

Today I ask for patience
Today I ask for joy
Today I ask for presence
All tools I can employ

Today I will be tested
Today I will succeed
Today I will have triumph
If I have all the things I need

Today I will give stillness
Today I will give hope
Today I will give clarity
To help other people cope

LAUGHTER

Laughter a bubbly feeling
To me the key to all healing

Why do I have the uncontrollable urge to giggle?
A soul-shaking one that will be sure to make me jiggle

Ha ha ha he he he
Something is so funny to me

Laughter is a vent to end frustration
Laughter is a most enjoyable sensation

To laugh, to giggle, to be at peace
Laughter to me is a form of release

MY SPIRIT

My spiritual soul is alive
I'm seeing the signs
You're talking to me
Making yourself known
I'm noticing
All the signs that you've shown

I had silenced you before
Afraid of the truth
Afraid of my majesty
Foolish in youth

Afraid to take my crown

But now I am ready
You've made me the queen
Queen of my destiny
Leader of the pack
Ascended to greatness
Not fiction
A fact

Time to take my place
Make the world change
I am majestic
I am powerful
I am unapologetically, spiritually ME

CLOTHES

Are clothes protective or preventative?
Are clothes covering or chastisement?
I just don't know
I wear them
So do you

DREAMS

I enjoy dreaming
Dreaming is a welcome escape
From the mundane routine of life
I think that I spend more time in Dreamland than in reality
Dreams are not only nocturnal visitors
I also and often entertain them by daylight
The key I believe to understanding and accepting dreams is
being able to categorise them.
Realisable dreams or fantasies
There are also good dreams and bad dreams
I control good dreams
My subconscious controls the bad ones

PASSION ONE

One of the passions of my life is music
Not any particular music just the thing as a whole
Different types of music have the ability to set or change my
mood
I have very set ideas about music and its suitability for
occasions
Is this obsession?
No, just passion

PASSION TWO

Another passion of mine is writing
Being able to catch a mood on paper for posterity
The ability to write about one's feelings shouldn't be taken lightly
I can only write when I am taken with a mood.
Generally melancholy or hyperactivity.
Is this obsession?
No, just passion

LIFE

What is life?
A circle?
A square?
If it is a circle then I'd say
This is good and bad
Forever going around
Experiencing the same things over and again in different forms.
Learning from mistakes yet feeling trapped in repetition

A square however, makes one feel boxed in.
Always coming to a corner or edge.
Yet there is always the choice of another plane
Life is good
Life is bad

HOME

Where is home?
They say home is where the heart is
How wrong they are
My heart is within my body
My body is not home
Home is where the heart belongs
And where the spirit and soul are
Home for me is a six letter word
And I miss it

MUSIC

The beat
The rhythm
The soul

Missy Elliott
Whitney Houston
Nat King Cole

The new
The now
The old

All worth
To me
Their weight
In gold

ADULTERY

Exactly what is betrayal?
In a relationship most people define betrayal as the act of
adultery.
That seems to be the thing that gets the most air time.
But what is it about adultery that gets us so angry?

For me it isn't necessarily the act
It's the lies, the consequences and eventual mistrust
The what if of what he might be doing when he isn't with me.

It's the bitter after taste.

DREAMCATCHER

She stands in her majesty
Back straight and tall
Hair should be upswept
But she lets it fall
Warrior Princess
My dreams are her crown
My lover, my savior
She won't let me down
She is my hero
She is my muse
With her by my side
I will win
I can't lose

GYM BUNNY

Gym bunny gym bunny
Look at you
Trussed up in lycra
Laces tied
Time to work on the butt
Time to work on the thighs

Gym bunny gym bunny
What do you eat?
Looks like the food
Must go to your feet

PUPPY LOVE

Ahh the joys of puppy love
When how we loved was simple
When most important criteria
Was does he have a dimple

Puppy love is very cute
All hearts and smiles and flowers
It takes your heart and gives you light
But intellect gets devoured

FAT GIRL

Fat girl they said
As I slowly walked by
Head in the air
I tried not to cry

Fat girl they taunted
Determined to tease
I wanted to say
Stop taunting me please

But I walked silently on
Back stiff and straight
I have things to do
Don't want to be late

They taunt me now
Think that I care
They don't know
I have knowledge to share

I'm smart and I'm funny
I'm not my weight
In a few years
It's me they'll want to date

I'm headed for greatness
A life full of joys
But them on the street
Will likely stay boys

PRETTY HAIR

Look at all that pretty hair
Falling off your head
Curls all tousled hanging loose
Like you've just rolled out of bed

Look at all that pretty hair
They tell me all the time
Like I care about it all
Without it I'd be fine

She used to have such pretty hair
They say to me complaining
I've chopped it all completely off
There's none of it remaining

She'll never have such pretty hair
Like when she was much younger
It can't grow back much more than that
Don't think it can get longer

The jokes on them
Cos I don't care
I'm glad I'm rid
Of my pretty hair

SEASONS

Seasons come and seasons go
Weather goes from hot to cold

Leaves grow
Leaves turn brown
Leaves shrivel
Leaves fall down

The sun is bright
Then mute and dark
Winter bites
No time for the park

Spring brings hope
And joyful laughing
No time for us to mourn
The winter's passing

CHRISTMAS

I've always loved Christmas the sights and the sounds. And the smell is amazing. The roasting of ham and the warm smell of pepperpot boiling on the stove.

Christmas represents a warmth and unity that is never replicated on any other holiday. All the meals at Christmas are amazingly tasty. And they smell as good as they taste.

But it's not just about food, it's about the colours and the visual aspects of Christmas.

Traditionally red and green with accents of gold and silver were my colours but as I have grown and developed my own zany Christmas spirit. I've created my own colour palette.

I start Christmas early. Pretty much from January 1st I am ready for my next year. My current Christmas colours are purple, silver, black and pink. If I'm feeling rebellious I throw some teal in as well, it's all about pretty colours offset by the deep green of my giant Christmas tree.

I also use wrapping paper to create a colourful scene in my living room. My paper must match my annual theme or else I'm not happy!

Christmas is my holiday.

I am HOT Mama Christmas x

WATCHING

I watch you from the corner of my eye.
Don't want you to notice me noticing you.
As you make strokes on the canvas
I'm mesmerized by the flex of your arm muscles.

You are so focused that you don't notice the bead of sweat
rolling down the back of your neck.
But I do

Your brush strokes are creating a vision in red
The colour of passion, fire and heat.
Seems appropriate, considering the interest that you've ignited
in me.
I only took the class to busy my mind.
Had no idea of what I might find.

I should be working on my piece of art.
But you and your piece have me mesmerized.
I've never even spoken to you
And it's already three weeks in.

But I know your name, it's Russell they say.
And I know that your lips are juicy like fruit
 And rich like the hue of a berry.
I know you have a dimple and a 1000 watt smile.

I must have closed my eyes whilst thinking about you
Because now you're next to me
Looking at me enquiringly.
You asked me a question
That I didn't hear.

"Pardon?" I say looking into your eyes
"Can I borrow some red?" you ask again
And I nod my head thinking you're definitely a TEN

CELESTIA

As stars align
And moons arrive
I feel a vibration
I feel more alive

My senses spark
And my intuition roars
Not long now
Till the rain starts to pour

I'm in touch with the weather
I'm a heavenly soul
As my mind starts to tumble
I hear thunder roll

Whenever I have
A decision to make
My mind clicks into action
Then the earth starts to shake

The connection is strong
Between me and the earth
I am part of her being
To me she gave birth

I'm controlling the elements
Just using my mind
Fire and water, are my strengths
You will find

Queen of the fire
That's what they call me in tales
The might of my power
Makes mere mortal hearts pale

As the storm passes

My powers decline
Need to settle in slumber
Till stars realign

Random Passages

These are the beginnings of stories that may or may not be published. These characters have captured my mind and I hope they capture yours as well.

The Gift

THE GIFT

Have you ever had the feeling that you weren't alone in an empty room? Ever felt a presence that you couldn't explain? Welcome to my world. I was about six years old when it started happening to me.

Any time that I was afraid I would feel like someone was with me. It was like an energy force. Present yet invisible. Somehow even at that age I knew that it was a secret. Something that I should never divulge to anyone because I didn't want to seem strange or weird. So I never told anyone about her. And I knew it was a her. Without any rational evidence to the contrary I knew that my "person" was a she.

As I got older the feeling of not being alone continued. "She" was with me whenever I was stressed or scared. I never felt alone.

But that wasn't all. As I grew up I found that I sometimes knew things that I shouldn't know. I remember having vivid dreams in amazing Technicolor. Seeing faces and places that were unknown to me consciously but subconsciously, they seemed as familiar as my own skin.

I was so confused. I would worry about whether I was crazy and wonder when I would next guess something that I shouldn't know. But as time elapsed, that worry turned into acceptance.

I became resigned to the feelings of déjà vu that frequently washed over me. I got used to playing conversations with my loved ones in my head long before they actually occurred. This became my normality and I was at peace with it. That is until the darkness descended.

When I turned 15, things changed. Suddenly I felt a sense of foreboding pervade every aspect of my being. I didn't understand it. It was as if overnight I was suddenly afraid of everything. Second-guessing my every decision and wondering why I had these premonitions. I became a virtual recluse and I remember that my headaches started at around this time.

Sometimes when I was in busy places I would feel like I was going mad. I would hear voices chattering away in my mind but with no clear pattern or distinction. It was just noise. I couldn't focus and my schoolwork suffered.

Then one day my Aunty Beth came to visit. She was my father's sister. I hadn't met her before but as soon as I saw her I felt a sense of calm wash over me.

Aunty Beth looked at me that first day. Her head cocked like a dog listening for sounds and as clear as day I heard her say to me "It's ok child. I see you. I know you. I'm here." But her mouth didn't move and consciously I knew that she hadn't uttered a word. Yet I also knew with equal certainty that she had spoken to me.

It wasn't until the next morning that we got the chance to be alone. I had woken up early to go into the garden. A habit I had developed months earlier when the headaches had started. The greenery was relaxing and no one bothered me out here if I woke up early enough.

That morning Aunty Beth was sitting there waiting for me. When she saw me she shifted down the bench and patted the space next to her beckoning me to sit down. I sat down willingly. My soul already at peace with her.

"You're struggling Lexi," she said. I nodded not sure what to say but knowing that she was right. She smiled at me and said, "it will pass. When I was your age I went through the same thing." "The same thing?" I said looking at her puzzled. "Yes" she said. Her mouth didn't move but I heard her voice.   "You heard that didn't you?" She said. Again there was no sound from her mouth, just a voice in my head. I stared at her puzzled and bewildered. "It's ok child; I'm talking to you telepathically. We're witches."

"Witches?" I said incredulously, "What do you mean?" "We come from a long line of witches" she replied smiling. "We are part of the Celestial Circle Coven and wicken blood has been in our family for centuries. It doesn't happen in every generation and it's been a long time since a new witch was identified in our family but here you are more than 20 years after the last one." "Who was the last one?" I said feeling overwhelmed and surprised. "It was me" she said with a smile, "It's how I can telepathically communicate with you. We are empaths. Those voices that you hear are the thoughts of everyone in this world. You have to learn to control it. To master it and to shut out the voices. So I'm going to teach you. Are you ready to receive The Gift, your gift?"

That talk changed my life. After Aunty Beth's visit I started to observe the things that I was experiencing and I recorded every time that I felt the "presence". It was more often than I had allowed myself to imagine and it felt good. But I was still curious. I wanted to understand my gift more than I did. So I called Aunty Beth and said "Aunty, I want to know more about the presence" she chuckled and said "when the time is right, all will be revealed" and somehow, even though I was annoyed, her comments made sense.

Years later when I was 18 I woke up from a nightmare. I knew that there was something wrong. I was going to lose someone. Then the phone rang………

Running

RUNNING

As I got out of the car I saw John and raised my hand to wave.
I didn't think of how I must have looked with blood dripping
down my arm. John dropped his shovel and came rushing
over. As he held me he asked what was wrong and looked at
me with such compassion that I broke down and collapsed in a
heap.

He picked me up and carried me to the house. By now Noah
and Nia, John and Shelly's children, were calling for their mum
as they had seen me collapse.

Shelly came rushing to the front door and said "What
happened?" "It was Ryan" I whispered. "Ryan?" she said as I
heard John muttering "I knew something was off about him,
I'm going to kill him."

John lay me on their sofa and I listened to him quietly cursing
Ryan and making threats to make him pay. Shelly nodded in
whole hearted agreement but still shushed him trying to focus
on me.

"Where is Ryan now Elly?" she said. "I....I..... think he's at work"
I replied. "After doing this? What kind of monster is he?" she
said. "He always goes to work afterwards" I replied
absentmindedly. "He's done this before?" she asked looking
horrified. "Yes" I replied shamefacedly whilst lifting my t-shirt
to show her the latest range of bruises and cuts that I had been
hiding for the past few months.

Her sharp intake of breath told me just how bad I had let it get
and it strengthened my resolve to run away and start a new
life. "I'm leaving Shelly" I said. "I need to get away." "Yes you
do" she replied tears springing from her eyes. Wordlessly she
offered me her hand and led me up to the bathroom.

In the bathroom she cleaned and bandaged my arm. We didn't speak much. We didn't need to. We were both distraught and no words could help. Softly she said "I never knew Elly, I'm sorry I wasn't there for you." I smiled shakily at her and squeezed her hand reassuringly. "How could you know?" I said. "I hid it well. No one knows. I barely knew myself. I never wanted to believe that he was capable of these things."

Shelly wiped her tear filled eyes and said "let me get you some clean clothes and a towel. Take a shower it will make you feel better."

As I stared at myself in the mirror I saw the woman that Ryan had made me. Long hair, manicured and pedicured nails and small pieces of expensive but bland jewellery. I wanted to destroy this woman and reclaim myself.

I opened the bathroom cabinet and took out the scissors. I held my ponytail out away from me and chopped it off in one cut. As it fell to the floor I felt a deep sense of relief and I smiled. I hadn't truly smiled for almost three years.

I took a brush, tousled my hair and picked up a discarded head scarf from Shelly's cabinet. I wrapped my head and started to feel like a different woman.

Finally Free?

FINALLY FREE?

As she lay on the floor battered and bruised she absentmindedly wiggled her fingers pondering the situation she was in. Where had it all started? How had she ended up being this broken bloodied woman? She rested her head on the cool floor as she reminisced about the past........

One afternoon on her way to class she had noticed him looking at her. His curly hair and piercing grey eyes caught her attention but she was late and couldn't acknowledge his warm smile. She hurriedly checked the time and strode up the street. A few minutes later she was surprised to hear running behind her. "Hi, I'm Jason," he said as he caught up with her. She ignored him and continued walking.

 "Don't you speak?" he asked looking at her puzzled. She sighed and said "I don't have time for pretty boys." "Oooh, so you think I'm pretty?" he said laughing. "Yes I do and it's not a compliment" she replied. "I don't entertain boys who are prettier than me." "So you thought about entertaining me?" he asked, his amusement obvious. "No, I won't be entertaining you" she said with a flush. "Well I want to entertain you" he stated. "What's your name?" "It's Roxy," she said impatiently. "That's different" he replied, "I've never met a Roxy before."

"Look, I can't talk" she said, "I'm nearly at class and I have strict parents." "That's cool" he said "I'm usually on that corner. If you're passing again maybe we can talk?" She nodded already distracted because she was sure that her tutor had seen her talking to him and would pass the information to her mother.

When she walked into class she found out that her tutor, Ms. Gold, wasn't home yet. She breathed a sigh of relief knowing that her secret was safe.

It was a fortnight before she saw him again. This time he wasted no time in joining her and again she feigned disinterest.

"You're very pretty," he said. "I'm sure you say that to all the girls" she replied drily. Compliments were rare for her. She was used to being called quiet and clever. Her sisters were both outgoing and glamorous which made her the family's "Plain Jane". "I want to talk to you properly" he said, "I'd like to get to know you better." "I'm not sure" she said hesitantly. "Like I said, my parents are strict." "I'm sure they aren't that strict" he countered.

She squeezed her eyes shut, trying to block out images of her mother striking her across the knuckles with a hot metal spoon because she wasn't typing fast enough to achieve an A grade in computing. "They are" she said quietly. "Well we'll just have to find a way" he said confidently "because I like you and I'm not giving up. Ten minutes, that's all I ask" he said, almost begging. "If you liked me you would make it happen." Her heart constricted. She wasn't ready to admit she liked him but already she could see her chance with him slipping away.

"I, I'll see" she muttered before saying "anyway I have to go, we're almost at the corner and I mustn't be seen." "Ok" he said with a disappointed sigh. Her heart hurt a little at the thought of losing what hadn't even begun. She trudged wearily to Ms. Gold's house but was surprised to see a sign on the gate. *"No class today due to an emergency."* It was as if her prayers had been answered. No class meant she might be able to see him, maybe snatch that ten minutes that had seemed so elusive just a moment ago.

She turned and walked back up the street looking for a glimpse of him. Just as she gave up she felt someone tug her hair and turned to see him smiling. "Why aren't you in class young lady?" he said with a pretend stern voice. "It's cancelled," she said. "So are you going to hang out with me?" he asked "I don't know" she replied. "I can't stand out here talking to you, someone might see me and tell my mother." "Well you'll just have to come to my house then" he said. She looked horrified but he said, "it's close by and my mum is home. It'll be fine."

He smiled at her beguilingly and the next thing she knew she was in his room.

His room was small and surprisingly tidy. A wooden desk inhabited one corner of the room and a sofa was in the other. "Take a seat," he said waving her towards the sofa. She sat down awkwardly wondering why she was here. "Would you like a drink?" he asked her. "Yes please" she said and he left her waiting in his room.

A couple of minutes later he came back with a glass of red liquid. "What's that?" she said. "It's cherry juice" he replied, "I thought we could share." "Ok" she agreed. He sat next to her and handed her the glass to take a sip. "Is it nice?" he said "yea really sweet" she responded. "So let me taste some?" he said with a sly smile. "Here you go," she said offering him the glass. "I don't want it from the glass" he said "I want it from your lips." As she looked at him confused he leant forward and kissed her softly on the lips. It wasn't rushed or probing he just kissed her lips and gave them a quick flick with his tongue. "Hmmmm yes that is sweet" he said and as she blushed she couldn't help wondering whether he was talking about her or the juice.

They spent the afternoon talking about life; he told her that his dad was dead so he worked part time as well as studying to be an electrician. She told him about her sisters and about her dad never being home because he was a policeman. She even disclosed her recent experience with the hot spoon. As he listened he took her hands and kissed them softly, uttering promises to protect her.

She checked her watch and regretfully explained that she needed to leave. He looked crestfallen and she found herself promising to return soon.

When she got home her mother asked about her day and she said, "it was ok." "You look very happy for someone who had

an ok day" her mother replied. She shrugged and said, "I guess
so." She didn't see the slap coming. "Don't you dare shrug
when you speak to me" her mother shrieked, "you're just like
your father, he shrugged as he left two days ago."

That night her dreams were filled with Jason. She imagined
him rescuing her and taking her far away where she would be
happy and free.

The next day at school was assembly day and as she walked
into the hall one of the younger boys handed her a note. She
looked at him confused and said, "What is this?" "It's a message
from Jason" he replied. She hurriedly opened the note and
found a scrawled message from Jason explaining that the boy
was his cousin, Luke, and that they could exchange messages
via him. He had included his phone number just in case she got
an opportunity to call him.

During the day she scrawled a note back to Jason saying that
she could meet him for lunch the next day. She hunted the
corridors until she found Luke and gave him the note. The day
couldn't go fast enough. She rushed home and went about her
chores, willing the evening to end so that she could daydream
in her bedroom. She was so caught up in her good mood that
she didn't notice that her mother was in a bad mood. She was
humming as she packed away dishes when suddenly she felt
her mother hit her across the side of the head, screaming,
"Would you just shut up! I can't think with you making that
stupid noise". She was almost seeing stars as her head
throbbed and the tears pricked at the back of her eyes. Feeling
hurt and angry she wished that she could hit her mother back
and not stop hitting her until she promised never to touch her
again. But this was all a fantasy, she silently continued drying
the wares and hoped that her mother was done with her for
the night.

As she walked through the school gates the next day Luke
handed her another note. Jason would meet her near his

college, which was five minutes away. At lunchtime she hurried to meet him. He was waiting for her and as she got closer, he walked towards her and smiled calling out to his friends "look guys, this is my girlfriend, isn't she a beauty?" She blushed and looked down, not used to being the centre of attention.

"How long have you got?" he asked. "I have a free period after lunch, so I can be gone for an hour and a half" she replied. "That's good we can go to my house," he said. He held her hand as they walked to his house and she enjoyed feeling his warmth.

When they got to his house it was empty. "My mum is at work" he volunteered. As she hesitated, he smiled and said "it's ok, you can trust me." And as he flashed his 1000-watt smile at her she realised that she really did trust him.

He quickly made them lunch and they sat in the kitchen eating and making jokes. She got crumbs all over her face and he lovingly brushed them off. It seemed so natural the way he touched her and when he leaned in to kiss her she welcomed it.

He kissed her gently, slowly invading her mouth with his tongue but the invasion was welcome rather than forced. He was nothing like the horny boys from school. The way he kissed her felt special, not sinful the way her mother described what "young people" got up to.

For six months they spent every lunchtime together. She was careful not to be late back to school so there was nothing to trigger contact with her parents and over those months their relationship slowly progressed from kissing to heavy petting.

Jason wasn't at all insistent about them having sex, he told her that she was special and he could wait because they would be together forever. Every time he said forever she felt warm inside, he was going to save her from her miserable home life.

A life punctuated by her parents' arguments and her mother's violent outbursts.

Then one day her world changed. She came home to find the house full of relatives. Her eldest sister Anthea was sitting at the kitchen table talking to her Aunt Jackie. As she walked in Anthea grabbed her in a hug and started to sob. "It's Daddy" she said "he's been in a terrible accident, we don't know whether he will live, Mum is at the hospital with Amy". She didn't know what she would do if her beloved father died.

Because he wasn't around much she worshipped him like a mythical deity and she couldn't make sense of her world if he was no longer in it. She felt lost and instinctively picked up the cordless phone and went to her room to dial Jason's number. "J it's me" she said when he answered, "It's my Daddy, he's hurt, and I don't know if he'll live". "Oh baby" he said, "I wish you were here for me to hold you and make you feel better". "Me too" she murmured.

"Who's there with you? He said. "My aunts, uncles and Anthea". "Tell them you're going to Giselle's for a few hours and come to me". "Ok" she said. She walked into the lounge and said "Thea, can I go to Giselle's for a few hours? I need to get out of the house". Anthea looked at her with pity knowing that she bore the brunt of their parents' dysfunctional relationship and said "yes hunny that's fine, be back by 8pm ok?" "Yes Thea" she said meekly excited by the prospect of seeing her beloved Jason.

She went to the top of the street and flagged down a taxi. She gave the driver Jason's address and settled in for the drive.

"I have to be back by 8pm," she told him as they walked into his room. "That gives us almost three hours. Tell me what happened to your dad," he said softly as he massaged her neck and guided her to the bed. "He was driving and his car got slammed by a lorry. The car flipped multiple times. I don't know the extent of his injuries but it's bad" she said as she started sobbing in his arms. He shushed her, rocking her gently while moving her hair off her face.

Her crying slowed and as she snuggled into him she felt his lips softly planting kisses on her head and moving down towards her cheek. She didn't know why she turned her head upwards but suddenly they were kissing. This time, his kisses felt insistent. She pulled away from him feeling confused and said "this is wrong, my dad ......?" "Fine" he said petulantly "I understand that your dad is more important to you". "No, no, it's not that" she said and kissed him to keep him happy because instinctively she knew it would placate him. He kissed her fervently and she didn't stop him because she needed him. She might lose her dad and she didn't want to lose Jason too. That night she lost her virginity. Jason was gentle but insistent. Afterwards he was loving and sweet, helping her to dress and reminding her they would be together forever.

When she got home the mood seemed lighter. Her mother had called, her father's injures although serious were not life threatening. He would have a long recovery but would live. She was ecstatic but slightly guilty about what she had been doing while the family waited.

The next few days were a blur. She helped around the house and went to her exams. She didn't remember the house ever feeling so homely. Because her aunts and uncles were in and out of the house her mother displayed a calmness and consistency like never before.

A fortnight after the accident her father was allowed home. His right leg was in a cast and so was his right arm so he needed lots of help. Her mother was happy, she had what she had always wanted, her husband home for longer periods. And because he was home more the violence disappeared.

About six weeks after her father's accident she was at her

aunt's office working as an intern when suddenly she felt light headed. The next thing she knew she was looking up from the floor whilst a number of concerned faces peered down at her.

As she tried to get up she felt light headed again and she recognised her aunt's voice saying "lie down and take it easy, what's wrong with you?" "I didn't eat breakfast Aunty" she said. "Well eat this" her aunt said as she pushed a biscuit under her nose. The smell of the biscuit made her stomach turn but she took a bite, grateful for something to eat. The rest of the day passed uneventfully and she left the office tired but happy.

As she made her way to Jason's house she felt ill again. She also felt exhausted. When she got there his mother let her in and she went straight towards his room. "He's just in the shower Roxy" his mum told her and she said "ok, thanks Mrs. Wilson".

She went into his room and gratefully lay on the bed. She must have fallen asleep because the next thing she knew Jason was shaking her saying "wow they must have worked you really hard." She smiled, rubbed her eyes and said "I don't know what's wrong with me today, first I fainted, then I felt ill, now I'm sleeping in the afternoon. I must be coming down with something."

As she finished the sentence, Jason grabbed the calendar off the wall. "When last did you have your period Roxy?" he said, "I dunno" she replied, "about a week before my dad's accident?" As she talked Jason was scanning the calendar, flipping the pages back and forth. "What are you doing?" she said to him yawning and rubbing her stomach, "I'm hungry". "You would be hungry" he said "considering you're eating for two".

"Eating for two? What are you talking about?" she said looking at him like he had grown an extra head. "Roxy you haven't had your period since we slept together the first time. We're going to be parents!" As he said the words she went numb. "No one gets pregnant the first time they have sex do they?" she said. He laughed and said "we'll soon see." He pulled on his shoes and said "I'm going to the shop."

When he got back she was still on the bed hoping that it had all been a dream. But as he urged her to take the test he had bought she knew it was very real. She reluctantly went to the bathroom and did the test. As Jason predicted it came back positive.

"So?" he said as she opened the door. She wordlessly handed him the test and he whooped with joy "Mum" he shouted down the hall, "Roxy is pregnant." As he ushered her into the living room, his mum turned smiling and said "That's great news, Jason needs the stability of a family and he'll make a great dad. I'll help if I can. When are you going to tell your mother?"

"Let's go tell your mum now" said Jason. "I don't think I should tell her yet" she said "there's a lot going on with my dad." "So your family is more important than our family huh Roxy?" Jason said "No, it's not that" "well it feels like that" he replied. "Ok fine" she said tired and fearful of losing him. Maybe it would be better if she took him with her.

Together they made their way to her house. The closer they got the more nervous she felt but Jason reassured her that it would be ok.

She walked into the house with Jason behind her. As the door closed her mum called out "Ben is that you?" "No Mum it's me" she said. Her father was obviously out which was a bad sign. "Where's Dad?" she said. "He went out with your Uncle John. I had hoped he would be back by now. Who's that behind you Roxy?" said her mother while suspiciously eying Jason. "This is Jason mum, he's my....." "I'm her boyfriend" said Jason. "I love Roxy and I want to marry her. I promise to do the right thing by her".
In a flash her mother's face turned into a snarl. "The right

thing?" she said as she advanced towards them. It was clear that she was in a very bad mood. As her mother got closer she shrank away but it was too late. Her mother grabbed her hair and wrapped it in a vice-like grip.

"What have you done you stupid little girl?" her mother shrieked while twisting her ponytail round and round. "Answer me!" She steadied herself ready for more of her mother's abuse but it didn't happen and then she felt her mother's grip loosen. She opened her eyes and saw Jason pulling her mother away from her. "Leave her alone" he said firmly. "Don't you ever touch her like that again. You're a monster." "A monster?" her mother said "what has she been saying about me?"

Like a flash her mother's mood changed again and she started to cry "I did my best with her, I'm a good mother and a good wife and this is the thanks I get. Well Roxy you obviously know better than me, you're a woman now. Get your things and leave." "Leave?" she said looking at her mother aghast. "Yes, leave, go and be with him, he is obviously all you care about". "No mummy, that's not true" she said imploringly. "Please let me stay, I'll get rid of the baby, I'll do whatever it takes." "No! Get away from me, you have ten minutes to pack." "What about Daddy?" she said. "Your father is too busy to be bothered with an ungrateful girl like you. He needs to focus on getting better not dealing with you." She started to cry and Jason said "Come on Roxy let's get your stuff. I'll look after you."

She blindly led him to her room and they started packing. She didn't want to take too much as she hoped it would blow over but Jason told her to take it all and promised they would bring everything back when her mother calmed down. She walked slowly down the stairs willing her father or her sisters to come home and save her from this latest nightmare but as usual she was alone to face the wrath of her mother.

They left the house and flagged down a taxi, travelling in

silence. She was curled up against the door of the taxi feeling nauseous, not sure if it was the pregnancy or the upset of the evening. When they got to Jason's house he let her out of the taxi and took her bag up the stairs. "Go to my room" he said "I need to tell my mum what's happening".

She went to his room and started to undress. She heard him come through the door and was shocked when he yanked her hair and turned her to face him. "You threatened to kill our baby Roxy, I heard you" he said menacingly. "I…I…was just trying to get mum to back down" she stammered. "Really?" he said. "Well it sounded like you love her more than our baby" he snarled. "Do you?" "No, of course not" she said. "Will you ever say something like that again?" he said as he yanked her hair harder. "No Jason" she whispered. "Pardon?" he said hitting her across the face, "No Jason, I'll never do it again" she said louder. "Good!" he said "Now get to bed, my baby needs you to rest."

She lay on the bed feeling like she was at home. By hitting her he had made it her new home in every way.

The next day she tried to phone her mother but she couldn't get through because the phone was disconnected every time she said hello. Her eye was swollen where Jason had hit her but his mother didn't acknowledge it and he was as loving as ever. She almost wondered if she had dreamt it.

A day turned into a week and a week turned into a month. Her family wouldn't speak to her. Even her aunts and uncles ignored her calls or promised to call back but didn't. She easily fell into a routine with Jason and was at his beck and call, condemned to this life by her family's rejection.

Now 10 weeks pregnant her stomach was rounder and Jason enjoyed rubbing it. Some nights she fell asleep snuggled in his arms and it was the warmest, happiest place she had known for a long time.

When she was about eleven and a half weeks pregnant her
exam results came out. She went to collect them while Jason
was at work and was overjoyed to find that she had passed all
her subjects. As she left the school she impulsively decided to
see if her father was at his favourite club. As she walked
towards the club he frequented she saw her Uncle John's car
outside.

She hurried into the club and was ecstatic to see her father
sitting at a corner table. As he looked up she saw that his face
was etched with disappointment. The look was like a physical
blow. "Roxy why are you here?" he asked. "I wanted to tell you
that I passed my exams." "That's good, but you should stay
away so that you don't upset your mother. Here's some money,
don't come back." She looked at her father suddenly seeing
him for the selfish man that he was. As he pushed the money
into her hands she grabbed it and ran out of the club.

She walked slowly back to Jason's house, bereft at this latest
rejection. She felt emotionally drained and wanted to crawl
into bed to sleep. When she got back to the house it was
empty. On her way to the bedroom where she planned to take
a nap she stopped to use the toilet. In the bathroom she found
that she was bleeding. She was scared but no one was home
and she didn't know what to do, so she went and lay down to
wait for Jason to come home.

About an hour later Jason came home. She sat up in bed and
felt an excruciating cramp rip through her. It was so intense it
made her groan and Jason asked what was wrong. She
explained about the bleeding and cramping. He looked
worried and said "let's go to the hospital".

At the hospital they waited for what seemed like an eternity.
The doctor asked them lots of questions and then asked her to
go to the bathroom to see if she was still bleeding. She came
back and told him that it looked like her period had started. He

then told them that she was miscarrying. They looked at each other shocked and Jason held her while tears streamed down her face, his own face streaked with tears as well. The doctor gave them some leaflets and booked her in for a follow up the next week.

On the way home she tried to hold Jason's hand but he pulled away. When they got into the house he turned on her, grabbing her and slamming her against the door screaming "this is your fault. You wished our baby away." She was weak from the miscarriage so couldn't protect herself. She slumped to the ground and tried to curl into a ball but he pulled her up by her hair and kept screaming at her that it was her fault while he pummeled her. He only stopped when his mother pulled him off her and told her to go and lie in the spare room and lock the door. She hurried to the room, locked the door and curled up in bed.

During the night she woke up feeling cold. She missed Jason's warmth, she got up and silently made her way to his room. She opened the door and watched him sleeping before slipping into bed next to him. He felt her next to him and opened his arms so she could cuddle him and whispered that he was sorry and that he loved her. She fell asleep grateful for his love and warmth.

The next morning Jason made her breakfast and told her to rest. As soon as she was alone she called her mum and blurted out "I've miscarried", hoping her mother would respond but the phone was disconnected again.

That evening when Jason came home she had cooked for him. He was all she had so she had to make it work. They spent the next few months mourning their baby and trying for another but when she didn't fall pregnant again she asked Jason if she could get a job and he agreed. She started work at a boutique and they settled into their life together.

They often argued and fought, the violence of their early days repeating over and over again. As she grew older and more disillusioned she returned his abuse and would bite or throw things at him. The months turned into years and their cycle of violence continued until it was interrupted by a telephone call.

She had been getting ready for work when she got a call from Amy to say their mother had died and the funeral would take place in a week. Jason was adamant that she shouldn't attend, telling her that her mother didn't deserve it. But she needed to go.

That was a week ago. She had disobeyed Jason and attended the funeral. When she got home he was waiting for her. He lunged at her and she remembered side stepping him so that he hit his hand on the door.

He was furious and so was she. All the pent up frustration of years of abuse had finally got the better of her. As he lunged at her again she pushed him away, hit him across the face and ran. She didn't remember how they ended up in the kitchen. She remembered fighting like a wild animal fighting for freedom. Freedom from a lifetime of violence. Her mother's death was the catalyst for her rage.

She shivered again, jolted back to the present by the cold. She was freezing. Her dress was ripped, she needed warmth. She crawled across the floor and snuggled into Jason's arms longing for his familiar warmth.

But this time there was none. His lifeless body didn't embrace her. Never again would he whisper he was sorry and that he loved her.

She had killed him.

She was finally free.

ABOUT THE AUTHOR

Ms. Paradox is an unapologetically open soul who has recently
answered the call to share her work with others.
Controversial, Curious and Commanding,
Her work takes you on a journey that you'll never forget

ABOUT THE PUBLISHER

ROI JELLY Publishing was established in December 2014 to work with writers who have a story to tell but want to retain control of their work.

We work with our writers to provide a bespoke publishing service that meets their needs and budgets.

We are anxious to hear from writers from across the world to discuss how we can help make their work go global. We are also passionate about bringing social issues to light and support various causes.

Find us at www.roijellypublishing.co.uk

****

VOICES OF NYA

Introducing VOICES of NYA. Have you ever experienced Domestic Violence, Sexual Harassment or Sexual Assault?

Do you know someone who has a story to tell?

Visit the campaign that we are working with to bring these stories to life

#EveryonesResponsible
www.facebook.com/VoicesofNya

www.ingramcontent.com/pod-product-compliance
Lightning Source LLC
Chambersburg PA
CBHW061033050726
47592CB00004B/1418